Direct objects can change places with indirect objects.

What's the difference between a direct and indirect object?

Indirect objects are usually people or animals.

SUBJECT	VERB	INDIRECT OBJECT	DIRECT OBJECT
I	gave	John	a book.
I	gave	the dog	a biscuit.

But don't forget — English is flexible! Therefore it is possible to change the positions of the direct and indirect objects.

SUBJECT	VERB	DIRECT OBJECT	INDIRECT OBJECT
I	gave	a book	to John.
I	gave	a biscuit	to the dog.

Notice that we now have to use the preposition **to**.

How do you know if an object is direct or indirect?

My dear boy! A direct object usually answers a **what** question. **What did I give? – a biscuit**. So **a biscuit** is the direct object.

2

TYPICAL MISTAKE

I gave ╳ to John a book.

The indirect object never has a preposition when it's before a direct object.

And now for a lovely exercise!

Exercise A Change the position of the direct and indirect objects in these sentences.

EXAMPLE

I bought some flowers for Mrs Grammar.

I bought Mrs Grammar some flowers.

Unfortunately you cannot change the word order in all these sentences so for goodness sake be careful!

1 I wrote my friend a letter.
2 I told a story to my students.
3 The student asked me a question.
4 I lent John some money.
5 I sang a song to Mrs Grammar.
6 Could you pass the salt to me?
7 They showed me the plans.
8 I asked him his name.
9 She read a story to her daughter.
10 I enjoy teaching grammar to my students.

Never put an adverb between a verb and its direct object.

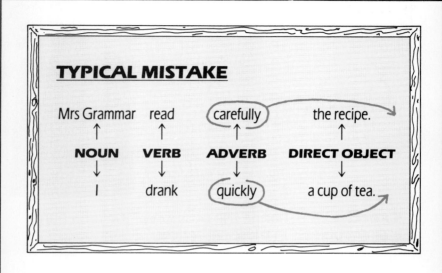

TYPICAL MISTAKE

Mrs Grammar	read	carefully	the recipe.
↑	↑	↑	↑
NOUN	**VERB**	**ADVERB**	**DIRECT OBJECT**
↓	↓	↓	↓
I	drank	quickly	a cup of tea.

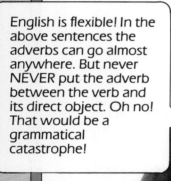

English is flexible! In the above sentences the adverbs can go almost anywhere. But never NEVER put the adverb between the verb and its direct object. Oh no! That would be a grammatical catastrophe!

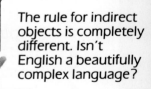

The rule for indirect objects is completely different. Isn't English a beautifully complex language?

Exercise B In the following exercise I want you to quickly put the adverb **slowly** in as many places as humanly possible.

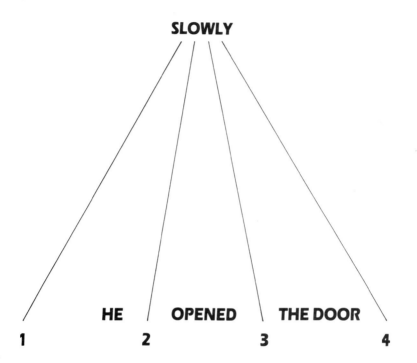

SLOWLY

HE **OPENED** **THE DOOR**

1   2   3   4

_____   _____   _____   _____

Exercise C Match each number to my comments on style.

he Opened St. the door

_____ Completely incorrect. A grammatical catastrophe!

_____ Jolly good!   _Heop, the door St._

_____ It's acceptable but a bit literary.   _Slowly he op. th_

① Beautiful! A masterpiece!!   _' He St. op th d''_

(gek. ?,!?!   _Slowly he op. th._

zie key

RULE 4

Adverbs of frequency <u>often</u> go between the subject and the verb.

RULE 5

Adverbs of frequency are <u>always</u> after the verb *to be*.

RULE 6

Adverbs of frequency should <u>always</u> go between the main verb and its auxiliary verb, or between two auxiliaries.

EXAMPLES

We always go to Sandringham on Saturday. (RULE 4)
He is usually hungry. (RULE 5)
I have never been to Budapest. (RULE 6)
I should never have listened to him. (RULE 6)

TYPICAL MISTAKES

I go always to the cinema. (RULE 4)
They usually are at home. (RULE 5)
I always have enjoyed singing. (RULE 6)
I never should have eaten so much. (RULE 6)

But some of these sentences aren't wrong . . . they're just bad style. Aren't they?

Yes! But don't you want to be stylish my dear?

6

What adverb of frequency is the best answer to this question? How often do you do exercises?

usually
rarely
often
seldom
normally
occasionally
hardly ever
always
constantly
sometimes
never
frequently

Constantly is the best answer, of course! Now here's another lovely exercise!

Exercise D Move the adverbs of frequency in these sentences if they do not follow my rules on good style.

EXAMPLES

It often is cold in Canada. (RULE 5)

I would never have known. (RULE 6) ✓

1 I get up usually at 7:00 a.m.
2 She is sometimes late for work.
3 John never has been to London.
4 We go often to the cinema.
5 I always have biscuits with my tea.
6 They always are happy to see you.
7 I always have been a keen gardener.
8 I have seldom seen such beautiful flowers.
9 You should have never told him.
10 I constantly am learning new words.

7

RULE 7

At the end of the line it's manner, place, time.

RULE 8

Travel verbs use place, manner, time.

RULE 9

Use the most precise adverb first.

EXAMPLES

	MANNER How	PLACE Where	TIME When
She sang	beautifully	at the contest	last night. (RULE 7)

	TRAVEL VERB	PLACE	MANNER	TIME
I	went	to Rome	by train	last year. (RULE 8)

	MOST PRECISE	
We arrived	at Bordeaux	in France. (RULE 9)
We got there	at 5 o'clock	in the morning. (RULE 9)

Exercise E Correct the word order of these sentences so that they follow my rules on good style. But beware! Two sentences need no correction.

EXAMPLE

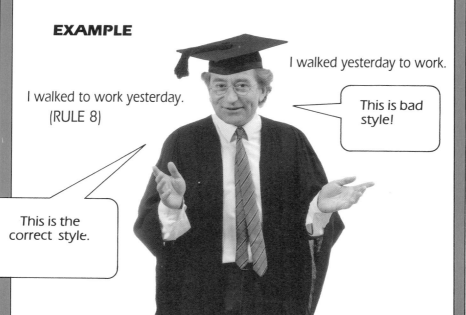

I walked yesterday to work.

This is bad style!

I walked to work yesterday.
(RULE 8)

This is the correct style.

1 1 worked in the garden hard yesterday.
   (RULE 7)
2 He is studying in Paris at a college. (RULE 9)
3 She goes by bus to the shops. (RULE 8)
4 He was born on the first of January 1950.
   (RULE 9)
5 We lived last year in Glasgow.
6 Who did you meet last night at the party?
7 They stayed last summer in Italy at a camp site.
8 Our team played in the match brilliantly on
   Saturday.
9 I travelled to Oxford by coach at the weekend.
10 I woke up in the morning at 2 o'clock.

OPSHACOM will help you remember the word order of adjectives.

OPinion **SH**ape **A**ge **C**olour **O**rigin **M**aterial

EXAMPLE

OP SH A C   O   M

It was a lovely little old brown English wooden table.

	ORIGIN	MATERIAL
It was a	wooden	English table. ✗
It was an	English	wooden table. ✓

	AGE	COLOUR
It was a	brown	old table. ✗
It was an	old	brown table. ✓

	OPINION	ORIGIN
It was an	English	lovely table. ✗
It was a	lovely	English table. ✓

Now of course you don't need to use five adjectives to describe my table! But OPSHACOM explains why some of these sentences are incorrect.

10

Now try this exercise!

Exercise F Eight of these sentences do not follow the OPSHACOM order of adjectives. Correct them!

EXAMPLE

He wore (leather) old shoes.

1   I bought a beautiful glass old bowl.
2   He drives a British new car.
3   They live in a big old wooden house on the beach.
4   I go to work in a red big bus.
5   She wore a beautiful blue woollen jumper.
6   It was a old wonderful song from the 1940s.
7   We had a picnic in a green large field.
8   We sat on horrible plastic orange small chairs.
9   Have you seen that British fabulous new film?
10 Please take off your old smelly shoes.

11

RULE 11

Adjectives of the same type should be separated by *and*.

RULE 12

When there are more than two adjectives of the same type, put *and* before the last adjective.

EXAMPLES

She wore a red and white hat. (RULE 11)
The red, white and blue flag was flapping in the wind. (RULE 12)

Don't forget the comma!

Exercise G Add **and** (if necessary!) to make these sentences correct.

1   I have a lovely black white jumper. (RULE 11)
2   The sofa was blue beige green. (RULE 12)
3   The tea was nice hot.
4   He likes British American poetry.
5   We had some delicious chocolate vanilla ice cream.
6   He has got a fabulous new car.
7   She wore a red white silk gown.
8   The hat was green red blue yellow.
9   They bought a large red green rug for their sitting room.
10   Last year I grew some beautiful red roses in my garden.

Adjectives (but not adverbs) can follow *be*, *become* and verbs of perception.

seems	sounds
appears	looks
smells	tastes

EXAMPLES

VERB	ADVERB		PERCEPTION VERB	ADJECTIVE
He runs	quickly.	He	looks	happy.
He sings	well.	It	sounds	good.
She cooks	brilliantly.	The soup	smells	delicious.

Exercise H Choose the correct adjective or adverb. Don't forget Rule 13!

EXAMPLE

Mrs Grammar looks beautiful/beautifully.

1. This pudding tastes wonderful/wonderfully.
2. Listen close/closely to the instructions.
3. He sounds angry/angrily.
4. I feel bad/badly about it.
5. He spoke loud/loudly.
6. Do you feel good/well about your new job?
7. I didn't feel good/well after I had eaten so many cakes.
8. John looked quick/quickly at his watch.
9. John looked nice/nicely in his new suit.
10. Those roses smell beautiful/beautifully.

Adverbs can be used before adjectives as intensifiers.

Intensifiers will make you lots of friends.

You're
beautiful!

You're
very beautiful!!

You're
incredibly
beautiful!!!

Intensifiers give adjectives more strength.

EXAMPLES

He is **unbelievably** handsome.
He was **terribly** late.
She works **incredibly** hard.
It was **terrifically** expensive.

Exercise I Which of these sentences are nonsense?

1 You were awfully nice to buy me lunch.
2 Mary is unbelievably truthful.
3 They were outrageously conservative.
4 We had terribly nice weather
on our holiday.

This is an
unbelievably
easy exercise.

I OR ME?

I is the subject.

The object is *me.*

Talk about the other person first.

EXAMPLES

I saw the dog. (RULE 15)
The dog didn't see me. (RULE 16)
In fact, the dog didn't see John or me. (RULE 17)

These rules are easy.

Yes! It's easy to make a mistake!

TYPICAL MISTAKES

John and ~~me~~ ^I^ went to the library. (RULE 15)

He spoke to John and ~~I~~ ^me^ (RULE 16)

^John and I^
~~Me and John~~ went to the cinema. (RULES 16 & 17)

TYPICAL MISTAKES

He is better than me. ✗ He is better than I am.

It was me who did it. ✗ It was I who did it.

Who is it? – It's me. ✗ It is I.

In formal written English (and examinations!) the rules are even more strict!

However, in everyday conversation such formal English should only be used if you meet a member of the Royal Family!

Exercise J Make these sentences correct in formal written English.

1   They spoke to John and I.
2   It was he who had the idea.
3   They gave the prize to me and him.
4   Mary and me went out to dinner last night.
5   He is fatter than I.
6   Me and John had an argument.
7   I and the others have decided not to go.
8   Were you trying to phone me?
9   The present is from John and me.
10   You and she should come over for dinner soon.

ME OR MYSELF?

RULE 18

Use reflexive pronouns when the subject and the object are the same.

You remember what the reflexive pronouns are, of course, don't you?

The subjects and objects are the same.

I
you
he
she
it
we
you
they

myself
yourself
himself
herself
itself
ourselves
yourselves
themselves

EXAMPLES

SUBJECT	OBJECT

I must stop talking to myself.

SUBJECT	OBJECT

He really hated himself for not telling the truth.

18

But please don't over-use reflexive pronouns.

Here the subject and objects are not the same.

Also reflexive pronouns are not normally used with the 'morning' verbs – **dress, shave, wash.**

I dressed ~~myself~~ in two minutes this morning.

Now try this exercise!

Exercise K Choose the correct pronoun. Use RULES 16, 17 and 18, and don't forget – English is flexible!

1   They held a reception for Mary and I/me/myself.
2   I was angry at I/me/myself.
3   He was angry at I/me/myself.
4   John and I/me/myself arrived late for the meeting.
5   I dried I/me/myself with a towel.
6   I shave I/me/myself with an electric razor.
7   John hurt him/himself playing ice hockey.
8   You should be ashamed of you/yourself.
9   I looked at I/me/myself in the mirror.
10 Everybody loves cricket. – Speak for you/yourself!

SINCE OR FOR?

RULE 19

Use *since* for a point in time.

RULE 20

Use *for* for a period of time.

EXAMPLES

How long have you been waiting?

I've been waiting since 2 o'clock.

You poor thing! You've been waiting for two hours!

20

This is a very common mistake.

Exercise L Choose **since** or **for**.

1 I have known him since/for a long time.
2 It has been raining since/for this morning.
3 I haven't seen you since/for ages!
4 I've been studying English since/for three years.
5 It's been three years since/for I began learning English.

SOME OR ANY?

RULE 21

If it's positive use *some*.

RULE 22

If it's negative or a question use *any*.

EXAMPLES

I have got **some** money. (RULE 21)
I haven't got **any** money. (RULE 22)
Have you got **any** money? (RULE 22)

Exercise M Only one of these sentences is grammatically incorrect – but which one?

1 I have got some good news!
2 Have you got any books about Britain?
3 Can I have some cake?
4 There isn't some cake left.
5 I don't know any songs by Vincent Van Gogh.

TRICKY!

Unfortunately these rules aren't very good. There are too many variations!

You can use **some** in questions if you think the answer will be yes.

Have you got some money? – Yes. I've just been to the bank.

And, if the question is really an offer, you can also use **some**.

Would you like some tea? – Yes, please!

Exercise N Again, only one of these sentences is grammatically incorrect – but which one?

1 This tea hasn't got some milk in it!
2 There aren't any tickets left for the show.
3 Have you seen any good films lately?
4 Have you got something to say?
5 Have you got anything to say!?

And is this sentence correct?

6 There's some man on the telephone for you.

Yes it is correct!

some has a special usage which is very common in tricky English examinations.

some is normally used with a plural or a collective noun. However, it can sometimes be used with a singular noun if you don't know its identity.

There's some man on the telephone for you.
– Who is it?
— I don't know. He didn't say.

PLURAL OR SINGULAR?

RULE 23

Nouns and verbs must agree.

This rule is easier said than done. There are three problems.

Firstly, you must decide if the subject is plural or singular.

Mathematics ~~are~~ *is* fascinating.

Some singular nouns have an **s** ending.

The police ~~is~~ *are* here.

Not all plural nouns have an **s** ending.

Secondly, it's not always easy to find the subject.

SUBJECT
A number of **people are** learning English.

SUBJECT
The **number** of people **is** increasing.

Thirdly, some words which describe groups can be plural or singular! – **government, team, committee, family, herd, group.**

My team is winning! – No! My team are winning!

The best team is winning. They are very good.

Do be consistent! This is bad style because you haven't decided if **team** is plural or singular.

Exercise O Choose a singular or plural verb.

1   The news is/are at 6 o'clock.
2   There is/are an apple and two oranges in the fridge.
3   Physics is/are fun!
4   Neither of the two cars is/are suitable.
5   Everyone is/are going to the party.
6   The committee has/have made their decision.
7   A number of changes has/have been made.
8   The number of changes was/were decided yesterday.
9   John is one of the students who is/are going.
10 None of the books is/are very expensive.

TRICKY!

INCREDIBLY TRICKY!

25

WHICH OR THAT?

RULE 24

Use *which* for things.

RULE 25

Use *that* for people and things.

Choosing the correct relative pronoun can be a tricky decision.

EXAMPLES

**RELATIVE
PRONOUN**

The book which   I am reading is excellent. (RULE 24)
The book that   I am reading is excellent. (RULE 25)
~~The man   which   spoke to you was my brother.~~ X
The man   that   spoke to you was my brother. (RULE 25)

Both **that** and **which** can be used for things. But personally I prefer to use **that** in spoken English and **which** in written English.

Try this exercise! Choose **that** or **which.** Sometimes both are correct.

Exercise P

1 The man that/which invented the telephone was Alexander Graham Bell.
2 Have you seen the papers that/which were on my desk?
3 The car that/which I bought broke down.
4 The woman that/which wins will be champion.
5 The team that/which wins will be champions.

TRICKY!

THAT OR WHO?

RULE 26

Use *who* in relative clauses that describe people and pets.

RULE 27

Use *that* with superlative structures.

EXAMPLES

The man that spoke to you was my brother. (RULE 25)

The man who spoke to you was my brother. (RULE 26)

He is the tallest man who̶ I have ever seen. (RULE 27)

that

WHO OR WHOM?

RULE 28

Use *whom* when it is an object.

EXAMPLE

RELATIVE CLAUSE

The man whom you spoke to was my brother.

OBJECT

SUBJECT

MAIN CLAUSE

28

Many people think the use of **whom** is old-fashioned in spoken English. I quite agree.

But **whom** should always be used in written English (and in English examinations!).

And now for another lovely exercise!

Exercise Q Use **whom** if it is the object of the relative clause.

1 She is the woman who/whom you should speak to.
2 She is the woman who/whom spoke to you.
3 He is a friend who/whom I haven't seen for years.
4 John Smith was the player who/whom scored the most goals.
5 Did you see who/whom took my pen?

TRICKY!

No relative pronoun is necessary in relative clauses which already have a subject.

EXAMPLES

SUBJECT
The suit (which) I bought is made of wool.
RELATIVE CLAUSE

SUBJECT
The woman (whom) he married is extremely rich.
RELATIVE CLAUSE

But the relative pronoun in the following sentence cannot be taken away because it is the subject of the relative clause.

SUBJECT
The man who spoke to you is my brother.
RELATIVE CLAUSE

Exercise R Take out the relative pronoun if it is not necessary.

1 The radio which I bought cost a fortune!
2 The people who were at the party were terribly nice.
3 The people whom I invited all work with me.
4 Have you seen the book that I put here?
5 Have you seen the book that was here?

But see the variation on the next page!

VARIATION

Rules 24–29 can be used with relative clauses which tell us important information. Without this information you won't understand the sentence.

Alas, these rules will not work with relative clauses which give you extra information.

You can still understand the following sentences with or without the extra information.

EXAMPLES

EXTRA INFORMATION

Vancouver, which is in Western Canada, is a beautiful city.

Vancouver is a beautiful city.

RULE 30

Relative clauses which give you extra information always use a relative pronoun but never use *that*.

This rule is only important for formal written English.

Notice that relative clauses which give you extra information always use commas.

EXAMPLES

The house, which was built in 1860, used to be a bakery.

William Shakespeare, who is Britain's most famous playwright, was born in 1564.

Rome, that is the capital of Italy, is a magnificent city. (RULE 30)

which

32

This exercise is for geniuses only!

Exercise S Commas can sometimes change the meaning of a sentence. Try to answer the questions about John and Mary.

My car, which is red, is lovely.

My car which is red is lovely.

1 Who owns more than one car?

Women who are bad drivers make me angry.

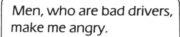

Men, who are bad drivers, make me angry.

2 Who is talking about the most people?

I have a friend, who is Irish.

I have a friend who is Irish.

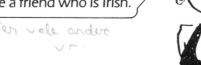

3 Who has the best parties?

33

TENSES MAKE ME TENSE

The present simple tense is used for permanent facts.

The present continuous tense is used for temporary facts.

I go to lunch at 1 p.m.

I always go to lunch at that time – it's a fact. (RULE 31)

I am going to lunch now.

I'll be back soon. (RULE 32)

I live in London.

It's my permanent home. (RULE 31)

I am living in London.

It's temporary accommodation while I look for a job. (RULE 32)

STRANGE BUT TRUE!

Rule 31 explains why you can sometimes·use the present simple to talk about the future.

EXAMPLES

My plane leaves tomorrow. (It's a fact.)
The course finishes next week.
The film starts in an hour.

If you wish, you can use the future simple in all of these sentences. Don't forget – English is flexible!

The course will finish next week.

Exercise T Are these sentences correct?
1 John is staying in London.
2 John stays at the Hilton Hotel when he's in London.
3 I am liking this music we are listening to.
4 I write a novel.
5 I am learning English.

TRICKY!

35

RULE 33

Use the present continuous tense to talk about the future.

The present continuous is used in 54 per cent of situations when people talk about the future. (According to a recent survey of the people who live in my street.)

EXAMPLES

I am having a party this evening.
We are going to Canada next year.
Tonight I am watching television.

The present continuous is used when we are talking about our plans for the future. So the following sentence is incorrect.

~~It is probably raining tomorrow.~~ ✗
It will probably rain tomorrow. ✓

Exercise U Are these sentences correct?
1 Tomorrow I am visiting the British Museum.
2 Our team is winning the match this weekend.
3 I am going shopping with Mrs Grammar.
4 I am taking my driving test tomorrow.
5 I am not passing my driving test tomorrow.

RULE 34

Use the present perfect to talk about what you have done.

RULE 35

Use the past simple to talk about when you did it.

EXAMPLES

RULE 34

I have been to Brighton before.
I have seen Hamlet 15 times.
I have finished my work.

RULE 35

I went to Brighton last year.
I saw Hamlet again last night.
I finished my work a moment ago.

Exercise V Which of these sentences is incorrect?

Concentrate on RULE 35. If the sentence tells you when something happened, then you must use the past simple.

1 I have studied English before.
2 Did you study English before?
3 I have been to university last year.
4 I have seen him this morning.
5 I saw him at 10 o'clock.

Turn to Page 60 for the answers but be prepared for a shock!

RULE 36

Use the present perfect to say:
how much you have done.
how many things you have done.
how many times you have done it.

RULE 37

Use the present perfect continuous to say
how long you have been doing it.

RULE 38

Use the present perfect continuous for
actions which have not finished or have
just finished.

EXAMPLES

What have you been doing?
(RULE 38)

I have been waiting for you.
(RULE 38)

I have been waiting for you
for two hours! (RULE 37)

I have waited for you ten
times this week! (RULE 36)

Exercise W Use either the present perfect or present perfect continuous in the following sentences.

Sometimes both tenses are correct. Remember – English is flexible!

1   I (write) a book for two years.
2   I (be) married recently.
3   They (win) ten games this football season.
4   I (play) the piano since I was a child.
5   How long you (work) as a teacher?
6   I (buy) 10 apples and 20 oranges.
7   I (listen) to a symphony by Mozart.
8   I (listen) to it many times.
9   She (learn) English for ten years.
10 She (learn) three languages.

RULE 39

Use the past perfect to express the superpast.

RULE 40

Do not use the past perfect for an action which is incomplete.

RULE 41

Do not use the past perfect if events are not connected.

SUPERPAST

PAST

NOW

I call the past perfect the superpast because the action happens before the simple past.

EXAMPLES

The party had begun before I arrived.

The past perfect is often used in reported speech.

He told me that he had spoken to John.

40

WARNING WARNING WARNING

The following sentences are a grammatical catastrophe!

They had told me that he went home.

Do you mean they knew he had gone home before he went home? How peculiar!

They told me that they had liked music.

Do you mean they have stopped liking music? Impossible! (RULE 40)

I had watched TV before I ate dinner.

The two actions are not connected. (RULE 41)

VARIATIONS

The final action is usually in the past simple.

The party had begun before I arrived.

But for some strange reason it is possible for the final action to be in the past perfect when an action has not been completed in time as in the above example when you were late for the party!

The party began before I had arrived.

There is no scientific explanation for this linguistic phenomenon. It's just one of the mysteries of the English language!

When two actions happen close together you will not have enough time to make a present perfect tense.

I ~~had~~ finished my work and went home.

Exercise X Not all of these verbs need be in the past perfect. Change the tenses.

1   John had told me that he had told you.
2   I had told him he had made a mistake.
3   I had turned on the television and had watched the cricket.
4   I had seen the film because I had read the book.
5   I had driven down the street and had parked the car.
6   She hadn't done well on the exam because she hadn't studied.
7   The questions had been harder than she had expected.
8   I had spoken to him before you.
9   The boss had asked for his work before he had finished.
10 Yesterday I had cleaned the house and done some gardening.

Do not use the future simple in a future time clause.

When we are talking about the future, future time clauses follow the conjunctions when, before, after, until, as soon as.

Use the present simple in these clauses.

I will phone you when I ~~will~~ arrive.

I will tell you as soon as I ~~will be~~ ^{am} ready.

We won't go until it ~~will stop~~ ^{stops} raining.

> Oh my word, it's easy to make a mistake!

Exercise Y Correct these sentences. Use the present simple in the future time clauses.

EXAMPLE

He won't finish the work until he ~~will be~~ ^{is} paid.

1 He will be angry when he will hear the news.
2 I will tell him, as soon as I will see him.
3 As soon as I will see him, I will tell him.
4 There will be dancing after we will eat.
5 I won't leave before you will.

> A TRICKY ONE!

Use *shall* for suggestions.

The use of **shall** instead of **will** is rather old-fashioned. I rather like it! In the good old days you used to use **shall** for:

PROMISES – You shall have a bicycle for your birthday.

PUNISHMENT – You shall have no pudding until you finish your supper.

INSISTING – I shall go whether you like it or not!

Alas, **shall** isn't used very much nowadays except for:

SUGGESTIONS – Shall we go?

Shall we have a picnic in the country?

Shall I open the window?

Exercise Z Here are some problems. Make some suggestions using **shall**.

1 I can't find the British Museum on my map but that policeman probably knows.

Shall _____

2 I'm hungry and it's lunch time.

Shall _____

3 It's noisy because the door is open.

Shall _____

4 That music makes me feel like dancing!

Shall _____

5 I'd love a cup of tea!

Shall _____

Oh what a good idea!

45

Use the subjunctive in advice structures.

> The subjunctive is another old-fashioned tense but I love it! My American cousins love it as well!

The subjunctive looks like an infinitive.

EXAMPLES

I suggested that he write to us as soon as possible.

He insisted that we not be late.

In British English you would probably add **should**.

He insisted that we should not be late.

Exercise AA In British or American English the following sentences are incorrect. Do something!

1 He recommends that John goes to the airport early.
2 It was suggested that he arrives two hours early.
3 It is important that he is on time.
4 It is essential that he checks in at Terminal 2.
5 I suggested that he took the bus.

Use the subjunctive in formal English.

Some people think this sentence is acceptable spoken English.

If I was rich, I would buy Buckingham Palace.

I completely disagree!

I know I'm old-fashioned but it's much better English to use the subjunctive after **if** and **wish**.

If I were rich, I would buy Buckingham Palace.

Exercise BB Some of these sentences would be incorrect in an English examination or if you were talking to me! Correct them.

1 If I was you, I would buy a new car.
2 I wish I was sitting on a beach in Brighton.
3 He was a very nice chap!
4 If he was here now, I would make him a cup of tea.
5 I wish the weather was better.

Use an *-ing* structure after *Would you mind . . .*

There is also a negative form of this structure.

Would you mind not stepping on my toe?

Exercise CC Would you mind making these sentences more polite?

1   Leave me alone!

Would you mind _____

2   Don't talk during the film!

Would you mind not _____

3   Pass the salt!
4   Turn down your radio!
5   Don't park here!
6   Lend me your pen!
7   Ring me back later!
8   Hurry up!
9   Repeat that!
10 Don't be so impolite!

You can never be too polite!

49

Do not use an inversion in noun clauses.

Most questions contain an inversion of the subject and auxiliary verb.

NORMAL

SUBJECT	**AUX VERB**	**MAIN VERB**
He	has	gone.

INVERSION (auxiliary verb before subject)

	AUX VERB	**SUBJECT**	**MAIN VERB**
Where	has	he	gone?

Noun clauses look like questions but never use an inversion.

QUESTION – What did he say?

ANSWER – I don't know what did he say. ✗

I don't know what he said. ✓

NOUN CLAUSE

Exercise DD Answer these questions. Begin each sentence with **I don't know**.

Beware of irregular verbs!

EXAMPLE

What did he think?
I don't know what he thought.

1 What time is it?

I don't know what _____

2 When did he go?
3 Where is he now?
4 How did he know?
5 Who told him?

TRICKY!

51

Use noun clauses in polite questions.

IMPOLITE

What time is it?

It's time you bought a watch!

POLITE

Could you tell me what time it is?

Certainly. It's 2 o'clock.

Good manners cost nothing – just an understanding of noun clauses.

EXAMPLES

With question words: **what**, **when**, etc.
When does the train leave? (impolite)
Do you know when the train leaves? (polite)

Without question words: use **if** or **whether** if there is no question word.
Has the train left yet? (impolite)
Do you know if the train has left yet? (polite)

Exercise EE Make these questions more polite. Be careful with the word order – remember RULE 47.

1 Where can I park my car?

Do you know _____

2 How much does this cost?

Could you tell me _____

3 Where's John?

Do you know _____

4 What time does the concert start?

Could you tell me _____

5 Are there are any tickets left?

Do you know _____

6 Where is the check-in?

Could you tell me _____

7 Was John at the party?

Do you know _____

8 Why are we waiting?

Could you tell me _____

9 Is it cold outside?

Do you know _____

TRICKY!

10 Who won the match?

Do you know _____

There are more questions than answers.

53

RULE 49

Do not use an inversion in *How come . . .?* questions.

How come? means 'why'. It is only used in spoken English but it is very common.

EXAMPLES

Why did you shout?

How come you shouted?

Exercise FF Change these **Why?** questions into **How come?** questions.

1 Why are we going?
2 Why didn't you stay at the party?
3 Why have you bought two identical jumpers?
4 Why did you do that?
5 Why are there no more more questions?

RULE 50

Negative and restrictive adverbs can affect word order.

When a negative or restrictive adverb is used at the beginning of a sentence there must be an inversion of the subject and auxiliary verb.

What!

Don't worry Wayne. It's easier than it sounds.

Negative adverbs:

never
under no circumstances
not once
at no time

Restrictive adverbs:

rarely
scarcely
seldom
only twice
only once in a blue moon
only once

EXAMPLES

I have never been so insulted in all my life!
Never have I been so insulted in all my life!
He seldom played his violin after 9 p.m.
Seldom did he play his violin after 9 p.m.

Exercise GG Rewrite these sentences with the adverbs at the beginning but be careful! Not all the adverbs are negative or restrictive so an inversion is not always needed.

1 I have never seen such a boring film!

Never _____

2 I have only once been in a Rolls-Royce.

Only once _____

3 I once wrote to the Queen of England.

Once _____

4 I seldom watch television during the daytime.

Seldom _____

5 I sometimes watch cricket.

Sometimes _____

6 John has rarely worked so hard.

Rarely _____

7 The village has not changed in any way.

In no way _____

VERY TRICKY!

8 The chairman is not to be disturbed under any circumstances.

Under _____

9 I have not played football since I was a child.

Not since _____

10 We can't begin the meeting until the chairman arrives.

_____

FOR GENIUSES ONLY!

57

ANSWER KEY

Exercise A

1. I wrote a letter to my friend.
2. I told my students a story.
3. NO CHANGE!
4. I lent some money to John.
5. I sang Mrs Grammar a song.
6. Could you pass me the salt?
7. They showed the plans to me.
8. NO CHANGE!
9. She read her daughter a story.
10. I enjoy teaching my students grammar.

Exercise B

1. Slowly he opened the door.
2. He slowly opened the door.
4. He opened the door slowly.

Exercise C

3. He opened slowly the door. — Completely incorrect. A grammatical catastrophe!
4. He opened the door slowly. — Jolly good! But be careful! If the direct object is too long there's a danger of bad style! e.g. He opened the large brown and white wooden door slowly.
1. Slowly he opened the door. — It's acceptable but a bit literary. This sentence would be effective in a suspense novel!
2. He slowly opened the door. — Beautiful! A masterpiece!!

Exercise D

1. I usually get up at 7:00 a.m.
2. NO CHANGE!
3. John has never been to London.
4. We often go to the cinema.
5. NO CHANGE!
6. They are always happy to see you.
7. I have always been a keen gardener.
8. NO CHANGE!
9. You should never have told him.
10. I am constantly learning new words.

Exercise E

1. I worked hard in the garden yesterday.
2. He is studying at a college in Paris.
3. She goes to the shops by bus.
4. NO CHANGE!
5. We lived in Glasgow last year.
6. Who did you meet at the party last night?
7. They stayed at a camp site in Italy last year.
8. Our team played brilliantly in the match on Saturday.
9. NO CHANGE!
10. I woke up at 2 o'clock in the morning.

Exercise F

1. I bought a beautiful old glass bowl.
2. He drives a new British car.
3. NO CHANGE!
4. I go to work in a big red bus.
5. NO CHANGE!
6. It was a wonderful old song from the 1940s.
7. We had a picnic in a large green field.
8. We sat on horrible small orange plastic chairs.
9. Have you seen that fabulous new British film?
10. Please take off your smelly old shoes.

Exercise G

1. I have a lovely black and white jumper.
2. The sofa was blue, beige and green.
3. The tea was nice and hot.
4. He likes British and American poetry.
5. We had some delicious chocolate and vanilla ice cream.
6. NO CHANGE!
7. She wore a red and white silk gown.
8. The hat was green, red, blue and yellow.
9. They bought a large red and green rug for their sitting room.
10. NO CHANGE!

58

Exercise H

1 The pudding tastes wonderful.
2 Listen closely to the instructions.
3 He sounds angry.
4 I feel bad about it.
5 He spoke loudly.
6 Do you feel good about your new job?
7 I didn't feel well after I had eaten so many cakes. – In this example 'well' is an adjective.
8 John looked quickly at his watch.
9 John looked nice in his new suit.
10 Those roses smell beautiful.

Exercise I

NONE of them!

Exercise J

These sentences are correct in formal written English:

1 They spoke to John and me.
2 It was he who had the idea.
3 They gave the prize to him and me.
4 Mary and I went out to dinner last night.
5 He is fatter than I.
6 John and I had an argument.
7 The others and I have decided not to go.
8 Were you trying to phone me?
9 The present is from John and me.
10 You and she should come over for dinner soon.

Exercise K

1 They held a reception for Mary and me.
2 I was angry at myself.
3 He was angry at me.
4 John and I arrived late for the meeting.
5 I dried myself with a towel.
6 I shave with an electric razor. – 'shave' is a 'morning verb'!
7 John hurt himself playing ice hockey
8 You should be ashamed of yourself.
9 I looked at myself in the mirror.
10 Everybody loves cricket. – Speak for yourself!

Exercise L

1 I have known him for a long time.
2 It has been raining since this morning.
3 I haven't seen you for ages!
4 I've been studying English for three years.
5 It's been three years since I began learning English.

Exercise M

4 There isn't any cake left.

Exercise N

1 This tea hasn't got any milk in it!

Exercise O

1 The news is at 6 o'clock.
2 There are an apple and two oranges in the fridge.
3 Physics is fun!
4 Neither of the two cars is suitable.
5 Everyone is going to the party.
6 The committee have made their decision. **OR** The committee has made its decision. – Be consistent!
7 A number of changes have been made.
8 The number of changes was decided yesterday.
9 John is one of the students who is coming.
10 None of the books is very expensive.

Exercise P

1 The man that invented the telephone was Alexander Graham Bell.
2 BOTH are correct!
3 BOTH are correct!
4 The woman that wins will be champion.
5 BOTH are correct! 'which' can be used with group words like 'team', 'group', 'committee', etc.

Exercise Q

1 She is the woman whom you should speak to. **OR** She is the woman to whom you should speak.
2 She is the woman who spoke to you.
3 He is a friend whom I haven't seen for years.
4 John Smith was the player who scored the most goals.
5 Did you see who took my pen? (The clause 'who took my pen' needs the subject pronoun 'who'.)

Exercise R

1 The radio I bought cost a fortune!
2 The people who were at the party were terribly nice.
3 The people I invited all work with me.
4 Have you seen the book I put here?
5 Have you seen the book that was here?

Exercise S

1 Mary. She owns more than one car, but she especially likes the red one. John has only one car. It is red.
2 Mary. All men who drive make her angry. Only those women who are bad drivers make John angry. Women who are good drivers do not.
3 Mary. Mary has many friends; one of her friends is Irish. John has only one friend. He is Irish. ↘ or she ?!?

Exercise T

1 John is staying in London. It's his temporary home.
2 John stays at the Hilton Hotel when he is in London. — It's a fact, but he's not in London now.
3 I like the music we are listening to. — 'like' is not used in the continuous form.
4 I am writing a novel. — It's temporary. You expect to finish it one day!
5 I am learning English. — All studies are temporary. Some day you will finish learning English!

Exercise U

1 YES: It is correct.
2 NO: Our team will win the match this weekend.
3 YES: It is correct.
4 YES: It is correct.
5 NO: I will not pass my driving test tomorrow.

Exercise V

1 THIS IS correct!
2 THIS IS correct! See the Appendix on American English!
3 I was at university last year.
4 I have seen him this morning. — Only if it is still morning!
I saw him this morning. — When it is no longer the morning.
5 THIS IS correct!

Exercise W

1 I have been writing a book for two years.
2 I was married recently.
3 They have won ten games this football season. (so far!)
4 I have played the piano since I was a child.
5 How long have you worked as a teacher? — How long have you been working as a teacher? is also possible.
6 I have bought 10 apples and 20 oranges.
7 I have been listening to a symphony by Mozart.
8 I have listened to it many times.
9 She has been learning English for ten years.
10 She has learned three languages.

Exercise X

1 John told me that he had told you.
2 I told him he had made a mistake.
3 I turned on the television and watched the cricket.
4 NO CHANGE!
5 I drove down the street and parked the car.
6 She didn't do well on the exam because she hadn't studied.
7 The questions were harder than she had expected.
8 I had spoken to him before you did.
9 The boss asked for his work before he had finished.
10 Yesterday I cleaned the house and did some gardening.

Exercise Y

1 He will be angry when he hears the news.
2 I will tell him as soon as I see him.
3 As soon as I see him I will tell him.
4 There will be dancing after we eat.
5 I won't leave before you do.

Exercise Z

1 Shall we ask him?
2 Shall we have lunch?
3 Shall I close the door?
4 Shall we dance?
5 Shall we have a cup of tea?

Exercise AA

1 He recommends that John should go to the airport early.
   AMERICAN He recommends that John go to the airport early.
2 It was suggested that he should arrive two hours early.
   AMERICAN It was suggested that he arrive two hours early.
3 It is important that he should be on time.
   AMERICAN It is important that he be on time.
4 It is essential that he should check in at Terminal 2.
   AMERICAN It is essential that he check in at Terminal 2.
5 I suggested that he should take the bus.
   AMERICAN I suggested that he take the bus.

Exercise BB

1 If I were you I would buy a new car.
2 I wish I were sitting on a beach in Brighton.
3 He was a very nice chap!
4 If he were here now, I would make him a cup of tea.
5 I wish the weather were better.

Exercise CC

1 Would you mind leaving me alone?
2 Would you mind not talking during the film?
3 Would you mind passing the salt?
4 Would you mind turning down your radio?
5 Would you mind not parking here?
6 Would you mind lending me your pen?
7 Would you mind ringing me back later?
8 Would you mind hurrying up?
9 Would you mind repeating that?
10 Would you mind not being so impolite?

Exercise DD

1 I don't know what time it is.
2 I don't know when he went.
3 I don't know where he is now.
4 I don't know how he knew.
5 I don't know who told him.

Exercise EE

1 Do you know where I can park my car?
2 Could you tell me how much this costs?
3 Do you know where John is?
4 Could you tell me what time the concert starts?
5 Do you know if there are any tickets left?
6 Could you tell me where the check-in is?
7 Do you know if John was at the party?
8 Could you tell me why we are waiting?
9 Do you know if it is cold outside?
10 Do you know who won the match?

Exercise FF

1. How come we are going?
2. How come you didn't stay at the party?
3. How come you have bought two identical jumpers?
4. How come you did that?
5. How come there are no more questions?

Exercise GG

1. Never have I seen such a boring film!
2. Only once have I been in a Rolls-Royce.
3. Once I wrote to the Queen of England.
4. Seldom do I watch television during the daytime.
5. Sometimes I watch cricket.
6. Rarely has John worked so hard.
7. In no way has the village changed.
8. Under no circumstances is the chairman to be disturbed.
9. Not since I was a child have I played football.
10. Not until the chairman arrives can we begin the meeting.

Exercise HH

1. I recently bought a car.
2. The letter just arrived.
3. Where were you?
4. Did you see John?
5. I just saw him.

AMERICAN ENGLISH GRAMMAR

People who speak American English never have problems with the present perfect — because they rarely use that tense! They use the past simple instead.

EXAMPLES

I have just seen a new film.

I just saw a new movie.

Exercise HH Rewrite these sentences using American English. Simply change all the present perfect tenses into the past simple.

1   I have recently bought a car.
2   The letter has just arrived.
3   Where have you been?
4   Have you seen John?
5   I have just seen him.

American and British people never have any trouble understanding each other even when their grammar is very different!

This book is based on the highly popular English by Radio series 'Professor Grammar'.

You can have a free English lesson every day if you listen to BBC English by Radio.

For a free schedule of broadcasts in your country write to:

BBC English (PG), Bush House, PO Box 76, Strand, LONDON WC2B 4PH

Editing: Stenton Associates
Design: Jane Evans
Cover design: Jim Wire
Illustration: Chris Simpson
Photography: Chris Perrett
Cassette production: Isabel Sargent
Stenography: Dawn Watkins

Typeset by Goodfellow & Egan
Printed in UK by Creative Print & Design

Professor Grammar would like to thank his dear friend Ian Bamforth, and, of course, Mrs Grammar. He would also like to thank his assistants Sue Broomfield, Nancy Gair and Wayne Morris.

© Doug Campbell 1991

Published by BBC English 1991
Reprinted 1991

BBC English, PO Box 76, Bush House, London WC2B 4PH

ISBN 1 85497 241 3